Welsh

It's Wales

Football
Heroes

Dean Hayes

First impression: 2003
© Copyright Dean Hayes and Y Lolfa Cyf., 2003
© Copyright of Ryan Giggs photo: Manchester United Football Club

Cover design: Ceri Jones
Cover photograph: John Peters

ISBN: 0 86243 653 2

Printed on acid free and partly recycled paper
and published and bound in Wales by:
Y Lolfa Cyf., Talybont, Ceredigion SY24 5AP
e-mail ylolfa@ylolfa.com
internet www.ylolfa.com
phone +44 (0)1970 832 304
fax 832 782
isdn 832 813

Contents

John Charles

Introduction

Many great players have worn the red of Wales since the Principality participated in its first international, against Scotland in 1876. While researching this book, the question arose, just how many players have pulled on an international shirt for Wales? It was a question that, while not impossible to answer, would tax the most dedicated of Welsh football followers. At the time of writing, it was 630.

The very act of running on to the park as a Welsh international ought, by definition, to confer hero status. These men tread where the rest of us can only dream. Yet, football is completely subjective and we all have our own ideas as to who are Wales's greatest footballers ever.

It is also a fact of human nature that we do tend to remember with most fondness the players from the era during which we spent our formative years. Consequently, I make no apology for the slight imbalance of my selection, which is geared towards the sixties and seventies, though I have been privileged to have seen all but a handful of the players mentioned within these pages.

There will inevitably be supporters who feel that some players who have been omitted should have been included ahead of others; that is a matter for healthy debate. If your favourites are not named here, they remain locked in the best place, anyway: your heart.

Dean P. Hayes

Pembrokeshire

January 2003

Goals are what football is all about and the great ones, like great occasions, live long in the memory, to be re-lived and re-told again and again. If there is one fact of the game which captivates the onlookers as much as the great goal, it is the great save. The ball speeds towards the goal-mouth, but in the very moment that the roar of the crowd reaches crescendo, a palm or a fingertip stretches out to divert it away. In that moment, one hero replaces another.

One of the most famous amateur players of the pre-World War One period was **Leigh Richmond-Roose.**

The son of a Presbyterian minister, he was educated at the Holt Academy, where he was taught by H. G. Wells. After taking a Science degree at Aberystwyth University, he began his football career with the town's club, his performances winning him the first of 24 Welsh caps.

In 1901 he joined Stoke as an amateur, though he proved to be a very expensive player to have. He paid little attention to the rules which his professional colleagues in the team had to obey. If the normal train service failed to meet his requirements, he would travel to away games by hiring a special train to himself, and arrive at the ground in a hansom cab.

He could punch the ball further than most players could kick it and although there were occasions when his genius proved erratic, it was compelling to see.

Dick Roose played for a number of clubs, including Everton and Sunderland, and once he signed to play for different sides, at different times, for different leagues. This led to one of the most famous incidents in the history of the Potteries derby. On 23 April, 1910, Stoke entertained Port Vale for a game that would decide the Championship of the North Staffordshire and District League. Port Vale's committee decided to take no chances and signed a number of notable amateurs, of which Roose was one, to bolster their chances. Vale was leading by 2-0 when the Stoke supporters invaded the pitch and carried Roose off towards the river Trent, in order to give him a ducking. Eventually, Roose, who claimed he believed the game was only a friendly, was released with the help of the police.

Roose once turned up for an international match in Belfast with his hand heavily bandaged. He told everyone not to worry, that he'd only broken a couple of bones but would be able to play. The photographers crowded around the Welsh goal just before the start of play, but once the game got underway, Roose calmly unwound the bandage and went on to perform heroics in a 3-2 win.

Roose's playing days were approaching their end when the First World War broke out. He was reportedly last seen on the battlefield by Gordon Hoare, the England Amateur international, and was officially reported lost on 7 October, 1916.

Jack Kelsey was a one-club man, though he was unlucky to be at Highbury when Arsenal players were nondescript in the extreme. He was the one world-class player at Highbury, and it was only he who stood between the Gunners and disaster. Yet, throughout that trying time, the presence of Jack Kelsey was truly formidable. His natural strength, honed during his teenage days as a steelworker, enabled him to withstand the attentions of men like Nat Lofthouse and fellow Welsh international Trevor Ford, in an era when knocking goalkeepers flat was an essential part of the centre-forward's art.

There had been a time when his future in the game seemed in doubt. After conceding five goals during his debut against Charlton Athletic in February 1951, Kelsey, the early part of whose career had been spent with Winch Wen of the Swansea League, returned to the club's Combination side, in an attempt to bolster both his confidence and experience.

He replaced the injured George Swindin for most of the 1952-53 League Championship-winning campaign, and it was not long before he made the Gunners' green jersey his personal property. Though there were no more honours for him at club level, he made up for this on the international scene. As well as winning 41 caps for Wales – then a British record for a keeper – he played for Great Britain against the Rest of Europe in 1955, and was one of his country's stars in their progress to the quarter-finals of the 1958 World Cup in Sweden.

Tragically, it was whilst he was playing for Wales against Brazil in Sao Paulo in May 1962 that Kelsey collided heavily with the Brazilian centre-forward Vava, and damaged his spine. At a subsequent medical examination it was discovered that he had a deformity of the spine which, had it been noticed earlier, would have prevented him from even playing League football.

His Arsenal days were far from over, however, as he took over the club lottery and shop and eventually retired as commercial manager in 1989, after over forty years at Highbury. Three years later, one of the game's most brilliant goalkeepers was dead.

Neville Southall is, for me, the greatest in a line of outstanding Welsh goalkeepers. His name was synonymous with goal-keeping excellence and, certainly, by the late eighties, his equal could not be found anywhere in the world. The one-time brick-carrier and bin man was a perfectionist, whose preparation extended to voluntary extra training sessions, minute study of the game in all its aspects and rigorous attention to detail, right down to practising with the precise type of ball to be used in his next match.

Like many of his contemporaries, Neville Southall was a magnificent shot stopper, but what gave him the edge was his ability to change directions at the last moment, sometimes even in mid-air, and an instinct for improvising unorthodox saves.

Everton had an early opportunity to acquire the services of Neville Southall but this was passed up and he left non-League Winsford United for Bury instead. A season later, his vast potential now evident, Howard Kendall recruited him for £150,000 and, by December 1981, he had replaced the more

Neville Southall

experienced keeper, Jim Arnold, between the posts. However, Southall was axed after a 5-0 drubbing at Anfield, and loaned to Port Vale. There were fears that the diffident youngster would not cope with this reverse but he returned from the Potteries with a new spring in his step and it was not long before he became the Blues' unopposed, number one keeper.

Two magnificent saves from John Barnes contributed greatly to the 1984 FA Cup Final win over Watford. At the end of the following season, in which Everton won the League Championship, the European Cup Winners' Cup and were runners-up in the FA Cup, Southall was voted the Football Writers' *'Player of the Year'*. He was only the fourth goalkeeper to be chosen for this title, following in the footsteps of Bert Trautmann, Gordon Banks and Pat Jennings. In fact, the Northern Ireland keeper once described Southall as a 'keeper without a weakness'. One save that season, from Mark Falco, which effectively ended Spurs' challenge, had experienced writers going back to Gordon Banks's famous save against Pelé in the 1970 World Cup for a comparison. His colleagues, though, were more blasé, saying that Nev made saves like that every week.

He also displayed great courage on countless occasions, diving in amid a mass of boots to catch low crosses. He suffered severe dislocation of the ankle and ligament damage, playing for Wales against the Republic of Ireland in March 1986, and it was wondered if he would ever get back to his brilliant best. Fortunately, he recovered in time to collect his second League Championship medal, as Everton won the title again in 1986-87. His part in one bizarre incident, a goal-mouth sit-in after he had walked out of a half-time harangue by Everton manager, Colin Harvey, did the big man less than credit, even though Nev is his own man and was acting out of frustration rather than malice.

Repeatedly, he was written off but, invariably, he made nonsense of rashly premature epitaphs by regaining top form, notably in the 1995 FA Cup Final, when Everton beat Manchester United 1-0.

Time finally began to catch up with the Welsh goal-keeping wizard midway through the 1996-97 season. Having made a record breaking 700th first team appearance for the Blues on the opening day of the season and received an MBE from the Queen in the Birthday Honours list, he found himself dropped for the first time in fifteen years, after the FA Cup upset against Bradford City. However, in the following season he established new records at Goodison. He was the first footballer to appear in 200 Premiership matches and to make a 750th appearance in an Everton jersey.

A free transfer led to stints at Southend, Stoke, Doncaster and Torquay before, in March 2000, at the age of 41, he returned to the Premiership with Bradford City.

As his Welsh team-mate, Ian Rush, said, 'For sheer consistency, there's no-one to touch Neville.' He was one of the finest goalkeepers in British football history.

DEFENDERS

Around the turn of the twentieth century, a defender was someone best described as a player who defended in his own half of the field. It was very rare for a player, detailed to occupy a defensive role, to venture over the halfway line and, consequently, those named as right-half, centre-half and left-half were basically classed as defenders.

Things slowly began to change. The line-ups started to alter, whereby one wing-half stayed back to defend, while the other was asked to go forward and back up his attackers.

Next, coaches attempted to nullify their opponents' style of play by introducing sweepers and markers, players who were put into the team to defend.

Therefore, in the last thirty years or so, certain players, although referred to as regular defenders, and who actually made the grade as such, were adaptable and were often placed in the team in unusual positions, wearing unexpected numbers, yet were still classed as defenders.

Fred Keenor, whose name was synonymous with Cardiff City during the inter-war years, led the Bluebirds to success in the FA Cup Final of 1927. The Ninian Park club had become the first and, probably, will be the last Welsh team to have won the coveted trophy. Keenor played for the club from 1912 to 1931, making 504 appearances, as the team rose from the Southern League to the First Division of the Football League before falling back into the Third Division (South).

The son of a bricklayer and mason, his rise to the status of professional footballer followed the conventional route when, after graduating from the schoolboy game to the local Cardiff league, he came to the attention of Cardiff City. However, just as he was beginning to establish himself in the Bluebirds' side, war was declared.

Sadly, the Great War scarred Keenor, both physically and mentally. A leg wound threatened to end his footballing career before it had even started. On being demobbed, he found work in a gasworks and on a milk-round before he rejoined Cardiff City.

The team rose rapidly, from the Southern League to the top flight of the Football League, and in 1923-24 just missed out on the League Championship on goal average; but it was in the FA Cup that the Bluebirds achieved greatest success, for after being beaten semi-finalists twice and runners-up in 1925, Cardiff City finally won the trophy in 1927. After that, the club's decline was rapid, and four years after lifting the FA Cup, Keenor found himself skipper of a team relegated to the Third Division (South).

Fred Keenor played an important role in Cardiff's successes during this period. Captain of both club and country, he was a rugged and uncompromising player, usually turning out at centre-half or half-back. His doggedness and determination made him one of the most effective defenders in the country. Such fitness levels as his required hard training, especially as Keenor was a heavy smoker and liked a drink. Quite often, when other Cardiff players were doing ball practice, Keenor was lapping the pitch in old army boots.

One of Wales's most courageous players, he injured his neck on the morning of the match against Scotland in October 1929. With Wales unable to call a reserve in time, he played with his neck strapped, enduring the pain in order not to let his country down. Also, whilst playing for his country against Scotland in the following year, Keenor was almost sent off for swearing at his colleagues but the referee showed leniency, accepting that he was so involved in motivating the Welsh side that he did not realise what he was saying.

Keenor stayed at Ninian Park for nineteen years, his ability making him a transfer target for other clubs, and though the Bluebirds had to sell several of their leading players, he stayed on until long past the peak of his career.

Though he still commanded respect, his old legs were becoming a liability and, at the end of the 1930-31 season, he left Cardiff to join Crewe Alexandra.

He briefly enjoyed some popularity at Gresty Road and, at the age of 38, added one final Welsh cap to his collection. He then moved on to become player-manager at Oswestry Town, before taking over a similar role at Tunbridge Wells, where he combined football with farming. He was later admitted to hospital with diabetes and this, coupled with the fact that he had been out of work for some time and so was unable to support his wife and seven children, resulted in the FAW running a benefit fund and making him a donation; such was the esteem in which Fred Keenor was held.

Brecon-born **Walley Barnes** was one of the greatest full-backs that Arsenal ever had. He was spotted while playing as an amateur inside-forward for Southampton, and he joined the Gunners in the summer of 1943. During the war years, Barnes played in every position, except centre-forward, including one match when he was in goal against Brighton.

At the end of the war, Barnes damaged his knee in a PT display and it was thought his career was over. However, with guts and courage, he fought his way back to full fitness and made his League debut against Preston North End in November 1946. He went on to win a regular place in the Arsenal side and, in 1947-48, not only won a League Championship medal, but also made the first of 22 appearances for Wales. Following an injury to Laurie Scott, Barnes moved from left-back to right-back.

During 1949-50, he captained Wales for the first time, and won an FA Cup winners' medal, when the Gunners beat Liverpool 2-0. Two seasons later, he played a big part in helping the club reach the FA Cup Final where they met Newcastle United. Sadly, in the 33rd minute of this match, Barnes tore his knee ligaments, when his studs caught in the Wembley turf and he twisted his leg. This injury kept Barnes out of action for the whole of season 1952-53 and, though he recovered sufficiently to play in the following campaign, his knee problems persisted and, eventually, in September 1955, he was forced to give

Roy Paul

up his struggle, and asked for his contract to be cancelled.

He had been appointed Wales's team manager in May 1954; he retired in October 1956 and became the BBC football adviser. He served the BBC in many capacities until his untimely death, at the age of 55, in September 1975.

Roy Paul was one of the greatest footballers to hail from the Rhondda during the 1940s. He began his working life in the mines, but it was his weekend performances for a number of local sides that attracted the attention of Swansea, who soon offered him professional terms. Sadly, the Second World War interrupted his career before the strong-tackling defender could make his League debut, and he had to be content with regular appearances in the Swans' wartime side.

Called up for National Service, Paul was posted to Devon, where he was invited to play as a guest for Exeter City. After an impressive display for the Grecians against Arsenal, he was ordered to report to his commanding officer, who arranged for Paul to go on a physical training course, following which he spent the rest of the war working as a PT instructor for the Marines in India.

At the end of the hostilities, Paul returned to the Vetch Field and, in 1948-49, helped the Swans win the Third Division (South) Championship. His performances during this campaign led to him winning the first of his 33 caps, when he played against Scotland at Hampden Park.

Whilst with the Swans, his career almost took an unlikely turn. He was offered £3,000 to join Colombian club, Millionaires, but decided not to accept. The Swansea Board were unimpressed by his trip to South America and placed the Welsh international on the transfer list. Not surprisingly, a number of First Division clubs were interested in signing him but, in the summer of 1950, he joined Manchester City, for a fee of £25,000.

On his arrival at Maine Road, Paul was appointed club captain and, in his first season, he led the club to promotion to the top flight, as runners-up to Preston North End. City reached the FA Cup Final in 1955, only to lose 3-1 to Newcastle United. After the match, Paul vowed that they would be back the following year, and so it proved as City beat Birmingham 3-1. In the close season, he brought the FA Cup home to the Rhondda, fulfilling the promise he had made to take the trophy back to the valleys, although, on one occasion, he awoke to find he had left his car window open and the FA Cup was still lying on the back seat.

By the time of the Maine Road club's 1956 triumph, Paul's international career had reached its conclusion; the highlight was a 2-1 win over England at Ninian Park, in his eighth and last meeting with the old enemy. Paul eventually left Maine Road, on the advice of a doctor, because his son suffered with breathing difficulties and it was felt that the air would be cleaner away from the heavily industrialised city of Manchester.

He wound down his football career with two seasons as player-manager of Worcester City, but found the strain of travelling from South Wales too great. On returning to the Rhondda, he became player-manager of Garw Athletic, and worked as a lorry driver until he retired in the mid 1980s.

Alf Sherwood, the master of the sliding tackle, was one of the best full-backs in the Football League and the one defender who could regularly subdue the legendary Stanley Matthews.

Alf Sherwood

He began his career with his home-town team, Aberaman, playing alongside wartime guests such as Dai Astley and Bryn Jones. It was whilst playing against Cardiff City in a War League game that Sherwood, who was playing at wing-half, impressed Bluebirds' manager Cyril Spiers, who signed him there and then.

During the rest of the war years, Sherwood turned out whenever he could get away from working down the pits. It was in a game against Lovells Athletic that the Bluebirds found themselves a man short at the back. Sherwood volunteered to have a go and, after playing as if he'd always appeared in this position, he stayed there for the rest of his career.

Alf Sherwood's pace, tackling ability and positional sense led to him winning full international honours for Wales, when he was selected to play against England at Maine Road in October 1946. That season he was a member of the Cardiff side that won the Third Division (South) Championship, and finished nine points ahead of runners-up Queen's Park Rangers.

Appointed as the Bluebirds' captain, he led the side into the top flight after they had finished as runners-up in the Second Division to Sheffield Wednesday. The popular full-back was also the stand-in goalkeeper for both club and country. When Cardiff travelled to Anfield for an end of season game in April 1954, the Reds had to win to retain their First Division status. The Bluebirds were leading 1-0 when Sherwood, who had replaced the injured Ron Howells between the posts, had to face a penalty taken by Scottish international winger, Billy Liddell. He saved it and Liverpool were relegated. In November 1956, he replaced the injured Jack Kelsey in the match against England at Wembley, and though he produced a number of outstanding saves, Wales lost 3-1.

Captain of Wales when they beat England 2-1 at Ninian Park in 1955, Sherwood left Cardiff in the summer of 1956, when it became clear that he was no longer included in manager Trevor Morris's plans. He then joined

Newport County, where he confounded his critics by playing in over 200 games and winning two more caps for Wales.

He later spent three summers in New York, in an attempt to promote the game in the United States, before he returned to these shores to manage Barry Town. On ending his involvement with the game, he worked in insurance before working as a security officer with the National Coal Board.

By the mid-1950s, **Mel Hopkins** was recognised as one of the best full-backs in the country. He grew up in a Rhondda rugby stronghold and, as a boy, had to form his own team in order to get a game of soccer. After being spotted by both Spurs and Manchester United, whilst playing for the Ystrad Boys' Club in Glamorgan, he was offered the chance to join the ground staff of either club.

He chose Spurs and rapidly developed, making his League debut within six months of signing as a professional. Fast and tenacious in the tackle, he eventually replaced regular defenders Arthur Willis and Charlie Withers, his form winning him the first of 34 Welsh caps in April 1956.

Hopkins became an automatic choice for his country, playing throughout the 1958 World Cup Finals in Sweden, when the Welsh were the surprise team of the tournament.

Although Ron Henry had been challenging Hopkins's place at White Hart Lane for some time, the long-legged defender was able to hold him off until he broke his nose when playing for Wales against Scotland in November 1959. Just as Spurs' famous 'Double' team was taking shape, Henry took his place and, despite remaining at White Hart Lane another five years, Hopkins was ousted and never able to get back in the team on a permanent basis. It was a cruel blow for Hopkins, who certainly would not have disgraced that great team. Though his loping gait made him seem awkward, that was a deceptive impression of an accomplished all-rounder.

After five years in the White Hart Lane shadows, he followed Bobby Smith to Brighton in October 1964, playing a sterling part in that season's Fourth

Division Championship triumph. The medal he received on that occasion was the least Mel Hopkins deserved.

He later had spells playing for Ballymena, Canterbury City and Bradford Park Avenue before becoming a sports instructor for the Brighton Education Authority and, later, he was appointed Sports Officer of the Horsham Sports Centre.

Mike England was a world-class centre-half, who most surely ranks as one of the best central defenders ever to play for Wales. He was fortunate to join Blackburn Rovers at a time when the Lancashire club had a successful youth side. In May 1959 he was part of the Rovers' team that won the FA Youth Cup, having made his League debut in the Lancashire derby against Preston North End the previous month. Unfortunately, the young England had a torrid time, as England international Tom Finney netted a hat-trick in a 4-1 win for the Deepdale club. However, during the course of the following season, England established himself as the club's first choice centre-half, and his performances over the next couple of campaigns led to him winning the first of his 44 caps, against Northern Ireland in April 1962. In fact, Mike England captained Wales on 28 occasions and, though he was never dropped, he missed a large number of games through injury.

In the summer of 1962, England was a member of the Welsh side that toured South America. In the game against Brazil, in front of a crowd of 140,000 in Sao Paulo, England was to mark Pelé. For eighty minutes Wales competed well but Pelé scored and Brazil ran out winners with a final score of 3-1.

Sadly, Mike England's time as an international player coincided with a Welsh side that, on the whole, performed disappointingly.

Frustrated at what he perceived as Blackburn's lack of ambition, he became increasingly disillusioned and, in the summer of 1966, after the Ewood Park club had lost its top flight status, he put in a transfer request. Spurs were anxious to replace Maurice Norman and signed England for a British record transfer fee of £95,000.

Mike England

In his first season at White Hart Lane, Spurs came third in the First Division but won the FA Cup. England gave a superb performance in the final, to dominate Chelsea centre-forward Tony Hateley. Although he missed the 1971 League Cup Final with an ankle injury, he helped Spurs win the 1972 UEFA Cup and the 1973 League Cup. He also scored in the 1974 UEFA Cup Final against Feyenoord, but Spurs lost over two legs.

Few forwards were able to get the better of the big, hard 'stopper' and, together with Pat Jennings, he provided the solid core to the Spurs defence that had been lacking since the early sixties. For such a big man, he was certainly amongst the most skilful of defenders, having the speed to recover should the opposition forwards pass him, and he was extremely strong in the tackle.

In March 1975, aged 33, troubled by ankle problems and with Spurs struggling against relegation, he suddenly announced his retirement, but then re-emerged in the following August to play for one season with Cardiff City, having spent the summer with Seattle Sounders. He helped the Bluebirds to promotion from the Third Division before spending a further four American summers playing for Seattle and appearing for Team America in the 1976 Bicentennial Tournament with England, Brazil and Italy. He also developed his strong business sense whilst in the States and this led him to establish a timber company in Blackburn.

Early in 1980, Mike Smith resigned as manager of Wales and was replaced by Mike England. His reign as manager had a sensational start with a memorable 4-1 defeat over England at Wrexham. His enthusiasm and commitment to the cause of Wales brought him great loyalty from his players and, in the course of his seven-and-a-half seasons in charge, Wales was desperately unlucky not to qualify for the final stages of the major tournaments.

An exemplary professional, who achieved respect and recognition as a top class centre-half, he also built a national team that had gained great respect in Europe by the time he left to develop his business interests and open retirement homes in Rhyl and Colwyn Bay.

Kevin Ratcliffe, a schoolboy team-mate of Ian Rush, began his career with Everton, the team he had supported as a youngster. After his first senior appearance, at Old Trafford in March 1980, where he made an impression by subduing the fearsome Joe Jordan, in a goalless draw, the young Ratcliffe spent two terms, in and out of the team. When he did play, for most of his games he was at left-back. Upset at being played out of his favoured position, he confronted manager Howard Kendall and, at one stage, there was talk of a move to Ipswich Town.

During these turbulent times, Ratcliffe won the first of his 59 caps for Wales, in a match against Czechoslovakia, marking the danger-man Masny and keeping him virtually out of the game.

Kevin Ratcliffe

In December 1982, his fortunes took a decisive upturn, when he ended a spell on the sidelines by replacing the overweight Billy Wright alongside Mark Higgins in the middle of the Everton back four. Within a year he had replaced the injury-ravaged Higgins as captain and, by March 1984, he was also leading his country.

In May 1984, aged 23, Kevin Ratcliffe became the youngest man since Bobby Moore, twenty years earlier, to receive the FA Cup. Within the next year, he led Everton forward to pick up the FA Charity Shield, the League Championship, and the European Cup Winners' Cup in Rotterdam, after a 3-1 win over Rapid Vienna. Thereafter, he captained the Blues to the runners-up spot in both the League and FA Cup in 1985-86, and to another League title in 1986-87.

Ratcliffe could read the game with instinctive shrewdness and was able to close down opponents instantly in moments of danger, often averting crises by clever positional play. His tackle was scything, when necessary, but he preferred to remain on his feet, well-balanced and ready to cope with any new threat.

In the spring of 1992, after appearing in 461 games for the Goodison Park club, he joined Cardiff City and helped them win promotion to Division Two.

In April 1995 he was appointed manager of Chester City but, despite taking them close to promotion on a couple of occasions, he parted company with the club and is now in charge of Shrewsbury Town.

MIDFIELDERS

During the early part of the twentieth century, the term midfielder was used to denote a player who lined-up in either the right-half (No. 4) or left-half (No. 6) position, or at inside-right (No. 8) or inside-left (No. 10). Generally speaking, a wing-half was the link between defence and attack and so, too, were the inside-forwards, although many of the latter were predominantly goal-scorers, yet several were included in the team line-up to serve as midfielders.

Then, as times changed and formations started to dictate a manager's thoughts regarding his team selection, so these types of players became commonly known as midfielders, pulling on shirts bearing numbers at variance with those their predecessors had donned.

The Nos. 7 and 11, in the past, were shirts worn by wingers. This is not so today and, therefore, one or two wingers are listed as midfielders, playing wide on the right or the left.

Billy Meredith was a phenomenon, a footballing freak, an ageing genius who refused to grow old and who, when well into his forties, was still able to make fullbacks wish they had never been born.

Probably Wales's greatest footballer, his figures are staggering. He played top-class football for no less than thirty years, from 1894, when, at the age of 19, he joined Manchester City from Chirk, his home-town just across the Shropshire-Wales border, until 1924, when he was accepted for every cup-tie in City's run to the semi-final. He played in 390 games for Manchester City and another 332, almost a career in itself, for Manchester United, between 1906 and 1921, scoring 150 and 35 goals respectively.

His international record is equally impressive. In the days when Wales's opponents were limited to England, Scotland and Ireland, he was selected for 71 consecutive matches between 1895 and 1920, but because of the demands

Billy Meredith

of his clubs, he was released for only 48 of them, plus the three Victory internationals in 1919.

Tall, gaunt and shambling, almost casual in appearance, he became transformed when he had a ball at his feet. His runs to the corner flag and the devastating crosses might be varied by his sudden cut inside for a shot at goal; he was as fast as he was skilful. When faced with a blanket of close-marking defenders, as he often was, Meredith's answer was as unexpected as it was brilliant. With a jink of his tall frame, he would lean right in to the would-be tackler, then accelerate past him; the tackler would give chase, only to find that Meredith had, with his jink, flicked a back pass to his own right-half, drawn off all the defenders and left the field open for attack.

As celebrated as the shot and the back-pass were the toothpick and the penalty. The first, rolled ceaselessly from one side of his mouth to the other, was a unique trademark throughout his career, all the more so, perhaps, for the fact that he never once swallowed one. The Meredith penalty was a piece of inspired and effective clowning. At the turn of the century, a goalkeeper could advance to the six-yard box, and Meredith was a master of looping the ball over his head.

Meredith's relationship with his two clubs was not as serene as his long service would suggest. He appears to have been an outspoken and headstrong young man, furious at his club's frequent refusals to release him to play for Wales, and disgusted with the miserable wages. It was money that led to his move to Manchester United in 1906, two years after he had scored the goal that helped City beat Bolton Wanderers in the FA Cup Final.

Eighteen City players, Meredith among them, were suspended for receiving illegal payments. Immediately after the suspension, he moved to United and within three seasons had won League and Cup medals with his new club. In 1921, a free transfer saw him back with City.

Two years later, the Welsh Wizard was called up to the City squad for the third round FA Cup tie against Brighton, and he played in the three subsequent ties. The semi-final against Newcastle United was Billy Meredith's last game for City. On 25 April, 1925, over 15,000 people attended Maine Road for Billy Meredith's testimonial. That day, a team of his own choosing played a combined Celtic and Rangers XI. The game, a 2-2 draw, was played with such panache that it was totally worthy of Meredith's achievements.

Ron Burgess was playing for his local side, Cwm Villa, when he first caught the attention of the Tottenham Hotspur scouts. He had signed amateur forms for Cardiff City but, with the promised trial not forthcoming, he took a job as a pit boy. After less than twelve months at White Hart Lane, he was told he would not make the grade. Before returning to the Rhondda, he went along to see the 'A' team play. They were a man short and he was asked to fill-in at right-half. He was a forward at this time but he obviously impressed, as Spurs offered him a place on their ground-staff and an amateur contract at the club's famous Northfleet nursery.

On turning professional, Burgess immediately secured one of the halfback positions and, over the next 15 years or so, was only absent due to injury, national service or international calls.

During the hostilities, Burgess was a reserve policeman, later leaving to work in a South Wales foundry. He joined the RAF, where he became a Physical Training instructor. When League football resumed in 1946-47, Burgess settled into the left-half position and became one of the finest attacking wing-halves the game has ever known. Possessing great stamina and a willingness to support almost every attacking foray, he could also defend solidly when the situation demanded.

An inspirational leader, Burgess captained both Spurs and Wales and, at White Hart Lane, was the energetic engine-room of Arthur Rowe's 'Push and Run' side that won the Second Division and Football League Championship between 1949 and 1951. The first Welshman to play for the Football League side, he also represented Great Britain against the Rest of Europe.

On leaving White Hart Lane, he joined Swansea as their player-coach, soon graduating to player-manager. After four years at Vetch Field, he took charge of Watford, leading the Hornets to promotion to Division Three. He later managed Hendon Town and brought the club to Wembley success in the FA Amateur Cup Final, before becoming Fulham's trainer and scout for Luton Town.

On leaving the game, he worked as a stock controller for a stationery concern in Wealdstone and was then employed as a warehouseman in South Harrow.

Roy Clarke's wartime performances for Cardiff City led to him winning a place in the Wales team for the Victory international of 1946 against Northern Ireland. Yet, after less than one full season of peacetime football for the Bluebirds, he was transferred to Manchester City.

Roy Clarke

He holds the unique record of playing in three different divisions of the Football League, in three consecutive games. His last game for Cardiff was the penultimate Third Division fixture of 1946-47, whilst his Manchester City debut came in the final game of their Second Division promotion-winning campaign, when George Smith scored all five goals in a 5-1 defeat of Newport County. Clarke's next game was on the opening day of the 1947-48 First Division season, when City beat Wolves 4-3 at Molineux.

During his stay at Maine Road, Clarke's left-wing play provided numerous chances for his City colleagues, Broadis, Westcott and Williamson. After being instrumental in City reaching the 1955 FA Cup Final, and scoring the only goal of the semi-final, he missed the Wembley showdown against Newcastle United because of injury. However, he was back at Wembley the following year, and picked up an FA Cup winners' medal after the Maine Road club beat Birmingham City 3-1.

He later played for Stockport County and Northwich Victoria before returning to his beloved Maine Road, to run City's Social Club for twenty-two years.

Cliff Jones began his career with his home-town club, Swansea, playing in the same team as his brother Bryn. He won his first full cap against Austria in May 1954, when just turned 19, and developed into one of the most exciting players in the game. Though he had to wait eighteen months before making his next appearance at full international level, it was worth waiting for, as he scored a memorable goal in a 2-1 defeat of England.

Just when it seemed he would leave the Vetch, he had to do two years' National Service, which had been deferred because of his apprenticeship in the Royal Horse Artillery (King's Troop).

By the time of his transfer to Tottenham Hotspur, in February 1958, he had 16 full caps to his credit, yet it was only after he moved to White Hart Lane that he began to train on a full-time basis.

A member of the Welsh side that did so well in the 1958 World Cup in

Sweden, he broke his leg during pre-season training, later that summer, but returned to become an indispensable member of the Spurs side, capable of playing on either wing or at inside-forward. Fast and direct, he possessed an elusive body swerve that left many defenders tackling thin air, and for such a slender-framed player of just 5 ft 7 ins, he had a prodigious leap. One of the most exciting sights in the game at this time was to see Jones leaving his marker for dead with an incredible burst of speed down the wing, flying like an arrow to meet a cross from the opposite flank, or soaring high above defenders to power a spectacular header at goal. However, perhaps Jones's greatest asset was his bravery; he was often courageous to the brink of madness as he threw himself, sometimes head first, at the flying feet of defenders if there was a half-chance of scoring a goal.

Cliff Jones

Terry Yorath

34

Jones was a key member of the famous Spurs team that won the 'Double' in 1961, the FA Cup in 1962 and the European Cup Winners Cup in 1963. He also picked up a third FA Cup winners' medal in 1967, as the first non-playing substitute.

Throughout his time at White Hart Lane, he continued to represent Wales, picking up 41 caps, and played for the Football League on three occasions, which was quite an achievement for a non-English player.

In October 1968 his great service to Spurs was recognised, when he was allowed to join Fulham for just £5,000. He won his final two caps at Craven Cottage before winding down his career in non-League circles.

He then returned briefly to the sheet-metal-working trade he had learned as a 16-year-old in Swansea dry dock. Later he worked at a Sports Centre before becoming games instructor at Highbury Grove School.

Terry Yorath was a tenacious midfielder with a reputation for being a hard man, and so it was easy to overlook the fact that he also had a fair degree of skill, essential for anyone who wanted to get into the great Leeds United side of the late 1960s and early 1970s. Yet, his entry into the game of soccer happened quite by accident, for he was more noted at school for his ability as a Rugby Union scrum-half. One day, he went to watch his soccer-playing brother play for Cardiff Boys against Rhondda Valley. The Cardiff lads were a player short and Yorath was pressed into service. He did so well that he went on to win four Welsh schools' caps at soccer. After turning down the two Bristol clubs and his native Cardiff, Yorath joined Leeds.

With the Yorkshire club he won seven Welsh Under 23 and 28 full caps, his first at full level being awarded in a match against Italy in November 1969, after he had made only one League appearance.

He took time to establish himself at Elland Road, moving up from a defensive utility role to become a hard-tackling, midfield ball-winner. A substitute in the Leeds 1973 FA Cup Final team, he made the starting line-ups for the 1973 European Cup Winners' Cup and 1975 European Cup Finals, but in all three picked up a losers' medal. He did, at least, collect some consolation with a League Championship medal in 1974.

In August 1976 he left Leeds to join Coventry City. Here he enhanced his reputation as a midfield destroyer and proved a fine captain, leading by example and winning another 20 Welsh caps, before joining Spurs in the summer of 1979.

He was signed to add a bit of steel to a Spurs midfield that, whilst boasting the talents of Glenn Hoddle, Ossie Ardilles and Ricky Villa, lacked a player who could go and win the ball. He performed the task admirably for a season, and added eight more caps to his collection, but was later allowed to leave and join Vancouver Whitecaps, where he won his final three caps.

On returning to the United Kingdom, he joined Bradford City, initially as a player, before becoming assistant-manager to his former Leeds team-mate, Trevor Cherry. He helped the Bantams win the Third Division Championship before he joined Swansea City as manager. Appointed part-time manager of Wales, he quit Swansea to take over at Bradford City, but soon found himself the centre of an acrimonious legal wrangle, that was only resolved when he bought out his own contract. He then returned to Swansea but left again, amid a further bizarre argument over whether he was sacked or resigned. He was then made full-time manager of Wales and, although he took them close to qualification for the 1992 European Championships, his contract was not renewed. He recently resigned his post as manager of First Division Sheffield Wednesday.

Leighton James was one of the most naturally gifted players in the British game since the Second World War, yet he could so easily have emerged as a Welsh Rugby international, excelling, as he did, at both the Association and Union codes during his schooldays. The son of a steelworker, James represented Wales Schoolboys before joining Burnley as an apprentice in October 1968.

Unable to prevent the Clarets' relegation from the top flight in 1970-71, his first season in the side, he was a regular thereafter, his sparkling performances

Leighton James

inevitably alerting the International selectors. He won his first Welsh cap in October 1971 against Czechoslovakia in Prague, the youngest ever Burnley international and one of the youngest players ever to be capped for Wales.

It was during Burnley's 1972-73 Second Division Championship season that Leighton James became a household name. His dazzling exhibitions of the winger's art stole numerous shows. After a couple of good seasons back in Division One, the Clarets began to struggle and, in November 1975, James was off on his travels. He joined Derby County; Dave Mackay paid a club record £310,000 for him. He was a regular at the Baseball Ground and was top scorer in 1976-77, but did not figure highly in County's future plans after Tommy Docherty took over the reins. Transferred to Queen's Park Rangers, he spent less than a year at Loftus Road before rejoining Burnley, whom he helped win the Anglo-Scottish Cup.

After Burnley's relegation to the Third Division, he was on the move again, this time to ambitious Swansea City. He was an instant hit and top scorer as the Swans finished third, to gain promotion to the top division for the first time in the club's history. He also played a key role in City's victory in the Welsh Cup, with its passport to Europe.

James moved to Sunderland in January 1983, and helped to spark something of a mini-revival at Roker Park as a slide towards relegation was arrested. He returned to the north-west in the summer of 1984, joining a Bury side with numerous Burnley connections. After a year at Gigg Lane, in which he helped the Shakers win promotion to the Third Division, he joined Newport County as player-coach. However, in July 1986, he returned to Turf Moor for his third spell with the Clarets, during which time he trod the Wembley turf for the last time in the Sherpa Van Trophy Final.

After coaching for a time at Bradford City, he became manager of Gainsborough Trinity and, later, Morecambe, before he became a regular broadcaster on local radio's sports programmes.

Robbie James was a 16-year-old apprentice when he made his Football League debut for Swansea. He went on to play in all four divisions for his home-town club, as they rose to join the elite. He knocked in 110 senior goals for the Swans as he matured from a hefty front-runner into a powerful Welsh international midfielder.

After Swansea lost their place in the top flight, James left the Vetch to play for Stoke City, but he was unable to reproduce his best form at the Victoria Ground, and soon another sizeable fee took him to Loftus Road and Queen's Park Rangers. Here he developed another string to his bow, by holding down a fullback spot, before he moved on again, this time to Leicester City. Seen as the sort of experienced campaigner who could help settle a predominantly youthful Second Division side, many of his efforts were negated by a lack of pace, and some of the vigour seemed to leave his game after Wales were eliminated from the European Championships. After a couple of lack-lustre performances in front of the Foxes' new manager, David Pleat, James was

Robbie James

allowed to re-sign for the Swans, and immediately assumed their captaincy, led them to promotion from the Fourth Division, via the 1988 play-offs, and scored in their Welsh Cup win of 1989.

Robbie James celebrated a further Championship success after joining Cardiff City, as they won the Third Division title in 1993, a season in which he also picked up his fifth Welsh Cup winners' medal.

His move to Merthyr Tydfil prompted the first instance of the FA of Wales convening a transfer tribunal to set the £10,000 fee, and he closed his League career on a total of 782 appearances, a total only ever bettered by Peter Shilton, Terry Paine and Tommy Hutchison.

James later played non-League football for a number of clubs, but died tragically while playing for Llanelli in a Welsh League match, when he was aged just 40.

Brian Flynn was first spotted by Cardiff City when he was playing for Neath Boys, but the Bluebirds let him slip through the net, enabling Burnley to sign him. He soon established himself in the Clarets' first team and, at only 19 years of age, won the first of 66 full caps for Wales in a 5-0 win over Luxembourg in the European Championships at Swansea in November 1974.

After the Clarets' relegation to Division Two, in 1975-76, it was always going to be difficult for the Turf Moor club to retain their up and coming stars. So it proved with Brian Flynn, who joined Leeds United, in November 1977, for £175,000, and immediately forged a superb midfield partnership with the great Tony Currie.

Instant control, constructive use of the ball and sheer endeavour made Flynn one of the best midfield players of that era, but Leeds of the late 70s and early 80s was not comparable with the vintage Leeds under Don Revie.

After a brief spell on loan to Turf Moor, he rejoined Burnley in November 1982, and played his part in the epic cup campaign of that season, which, nevertheless, ended in Burnley being relegated to Division Three.

He left for Cardiff in 1984, and, after spells at Doncaster and Bury, joined

Limerick as player-coach. After working on the Football in the Community Scheme at Burnley, Wrexham manager, Dixie McNeil, took him to the Racecourse Ground in February 1988. When McNeil resigned early in the 1989-90 season, Flynn replaced him as player-manager. After two disappointing seasons, he began to turn things around and, after Wrexham had beaten reigning League Champions Arsenal in the FA Cup, the football world began to take notice of the Robins. In 1992-93, he led the club to promotion to the new Second Division and, until his departure from the Racecourse Ground in 2001, he was one of the longest-serving managers in the Football League. He has recently been appointed Director of Football at struggling Swansea City.

Brian Flynn

Gary Speed is the current Welsh captain, a great competitor, who never gives less than 100% for both club and country. He began his career with Leeds United, where he became a regular in the side during the Second Division Championship-winning season of 1989-90. During the course of that campaign, he was called up as a late replacement to the Welsh squad for a World Cup qualifier at Wrexham, and although on that occasion he sat out the game on the bench, he did play against Costa Rica in the summer of 1990. That was the start of a long international career that has seen him win 66 caps to date.

For Leeds United, Speed had a remarkable League Championship winning season in 1991-92, when his forays down the left flank brought him and

Gary Speed

others, plenty of goals. Although he preferred to play a more central role, his versatility has allowed him to play in a variety of positions and, towards the end of that League Championship winning season, he replaced England international Tony Dorigo at left-back.

A courageous and gutsy player, he fractured a cheek bone in a match against Port Vale, but his commitment to the club was such that he returned to action only five weeks later.

In June 1996, Speed, who was once a paper boy for the most successful captain in Everton history, Kevin Ratcliffe, joined the Goodison club for a fee of £3.5 million. He enjoyed a dream start to his new career, scored on his debut against Newcastle and went on to record his first senior hat-trick in a 7-1 defeat of Southampton. The following season, Speed was named as the new Everton captain, and he responded to the added responsibility with some of the most consistently influential displays of his career. Though employed in a more central midfield role, he found himself acting as more of a tackling anchorman than he had previously been used to, but revelled in the role. However, midway through the campaign, there were rumours that he was unhappy at the club he had supported since he was a boy and, in February 1998, he was sold to Newcastle United for £5.5 million.

Obviously, his departure from Goodison was fractious, but he was prevented from giving his side of the story by having signed a non-disclosure agreement. Looking to pursue his ambition for more club honours, he was ultimately rewarded with a runners-up medal, following the FA Cup Final defeat at the hands of Arsenal.

During his time at St James' Park, Gary Speed has regularly turned in wholehearted and influential performances. An energetic player, who enjoys breaking forward to join the attack, he does not neglect his defensive responsibilities and is always ready to track back when the opposition has possession.

Ryan Giggs is one of the game's most talked about players and first came under the eye of Manchester United's fans when he captained England Schoolboys against Scotland at Old Trafford, at which time he went by the name of Ryan Wilson. He had been brought up in Manchester because his father, who was good enough at his chosen sport to play for Great Britain, moved to the area from Cardiff, to take up Rugby League after a successful Rugby Union career.

At about this time, his mother changed her surname to Giggs. Ryan was quickly recognised as something very special and was elevated through the ranks at a surprisingly quick rate. Giggs became the youngest-ever Welsh full international when he played against Germany on 16 October 1991, aged 17 years 321 days, and completed an unusual quartet of home country records for United. Duncan Edwards had become the youngest player to play for England; Northern Ireland's Norman Whiteside was the youngest-ever player to appear in the Final stages of the World Cup; and the youngest player to turn out for Scotland, Denis Law, also, later, played for the Reds.

Giggs set another record when he became the first player to win the PFA's Young Player of the Year Award in successive seasons, a feat he achieved in 1992 and 1993.

A winger who runs at defenders and goes past them effortlessly, to look for the cross, or to get on target with a tremendous left-foot shot, he has, during his time at Old Trafford, suffered his fair share of injuries: a broken nose, hamstring, broken left foot, but, fortunately, they now seem to be a thing of the past.

One of his best games for the club came during the club's 1996-97 European Cup campaign against Porto at old Trafford, a performance that was compared with George Best's legendary night against Benfica, some 31 years earlier.

On top of his form, there is no finer sight in football than to see Ryan tearing down the left flank in search of goals; one of the best came in the FA

Ryan Giggs

Cup semi-final replay against Arsenal in 1999, after a wondrous 60-yard run. Whilst United boss, Sir Alex Ferguson, enthused, 'It was a goal of genius,' Ryan described it as probably the best he has scored for the club.

Now United's longest serving player, the inspirational Ryan Giggs is well on his way to becoming the most honoured man in the club's history. Capped 33 times by Wales, he has won seven Premiership winners' medals, three FA Cup winners' medals, a Football League Cup winners' medal, and a European Cup winners' medal.

FORWARDS

All of the players included in this section proved to be prolific marksmen for both club and country and also created goal-scoring opportunities for their colleagues.

Swansea Town's first footballing hero was **Jack Fowler**, who played in a Vetch Field side that contained a number of the club's best-ever players: Billy Hole, Wilf Milne and Joe Sykes.

Born in Cardiff in 1899, Fowler grew up in a large family, with seven brothers and six sisters, and, like many of his contemporaries, he lied about his age and joined the Royal Naval Air Service towards the end of the First World War. At the end of the hostilities, he began his footballing career with Maerdy, and joined Plymouth Argyle, who were then members of the Third Division (South), in 1921. He was never given an extended run in the side during his time with the Pilgrims and, in February 1924, he left Home Park to join Swansea.

He made a goal-scoring debut in the home match against Southend United and, the following month, he scored the first of nine hat-tricks for the club, against Brentford. When the Swans played Charlton Athletic on 27 September 1924, Fowler set an individual scoring record for a League match when he hit five of the club's goals in a 6-1 win.

Though he was only capped six times for Wales, Fowler, nonetheless, managed to score three international goals, including two in a 3-1 Welsh away victory over England at Selhurst Park in March 1926, when the Swansea forward was at the height of his powers.

He helped the Swans win the Third Division (South) Championship and reach the FA Cup semi-finals during his time at the Vetch Field, and netted his 100th and last League goal for the club in a 4-0 win over Tottenham Hotspur in November 1928.

Like many other Swansea players of that era, he signed for Clapton Orient, and though he was appointed captain and scored a hat-trick on his home debut, these were unhappy times. On retiring through injury in 1932, he returned to run The Rhyddings Hotel in Brynmill. Though he later lost interest in football, he was happy to reminisce about his glory days with the Swans.

Trevor Ford was one of the leading forwards of his day, though it was as a full-back that he represented Swansea Schoolboys. During the Second World War, Ford served in the Royal Artillery and, with the unit team short of a centre-forward, he was tried up front by his sergeant major. After that he never looked back and, having signed for his home-town team, Swansea, in 1942, graduated into the Vetch Field club's first team towards the end of the hostilities. During the course of the 1945-46 campaign, he scored 44 goals in 41 games, deservedly winning a place in the Welsh side for the last Victory international of the season against Northern Ireland. Despite having a disappointing game, he kept his place in the side for the opening full international of the following season, and scored the first of 23 goals for his country in a 3-1 defeat of Scotland at the Racecourse Ground.

After scoring nine goals for Swansea in the first six games of the 1946-47 season, Ford became the target for a number of top flight clubs, and it was not long before he joined Aston Villa, for a record fee of £25,000. He scored nine goals in nine games that season, though his best campaigns were 1947-48 and 1949-50, when he found the net 18 times in each season. One of his best games for Villa came in December 1948, when he netted four goals in the 5-1 derby victory over Wolverhampton Wanderers.

Whilst at Villa Park, Ford had an offer to go and play in Colombia, whose sides were out of the jurisdiction of FIFA and so were able to pay much higher wages. He also received an offer from a top Portuguese club, whilst he was on international duty in Lisbon, but again he stayed loyal by rejecting the overture.

Trevor Ford

In October 1950, Ford left Aston Villa for Sunderland, the Wearsiders paying £30,000 to secure his services. He scored a last half-hour hat-trick on his home debut, as Sunderland beat Sheffield Wednesday 5-1. Ford netted a number of hat-tricks whilst wearing the red and white stripes of Sunderland, and scored four goals in a 5-2 win over Manchester City at Maine Road. In fact, when Ford was playing away from home, huge crowds turned up, not concerned with his powerful shooting and laying-off of balls but to see his bruising encounters with goalkeepers and centre-halves.

Dubbed by the *News of the World,* 'The most dangerous centre-forward in Britain', Ford soon became Wales's leading goal-scorer of all-time, netting a hat-trick in a 5-1 win over Belgium. He played against England seven times and only on his last appearance was he on the winning side, but his energy in those encounters, plus his four goals, made him a great threat to English supremacy. When Wales met England at Wembley in November 1952, the Welsh defence collapsed against the brilliance of Finney and Lofthouse, and were 2-0 down after just 11 minutes. England went on to win 5-2, with both Welsh goals coming from Trevor Ford. The first was, without doubt, the goal of the game, as he rounded Jack Froggatt before crashing a great shot past Gil Merrick. His second, one of the most treasured in Welsh football history, was a cheeky back-heel.

Ford later joined Cardiff City and, in his three seasons at Ninian Park, he not only found the net on a regular basis but boosted the image of the club and helped to swell attendance figures.

On leaving Ninian Park, Ford was banned *sine die* by the Football League, following revelations about Sunderland Football Club in his autobiography, *I Lead the Attack*, which was serialised in a Sunday newspaper. Though he was later reinstated, he was banned again when Football League secretary Alan Hardaker uncovered an illegal payment of £100 by Sunderland to Ford.

He then went abroad and spent four highly successful years in Holland with PSV Eindhoven. After the suspension was lifted, he returned to play for

Newport County and, later, non-League Romford, before a knee injury curtailed his playing career.

John Charles is probably the greatest Welsh player of all-time. He dominated games with Leeds United, Juventus and Wales.

He joined Juventus when they were an Italian League flop, and led them immediately to the title with his ability to score against packed defences. When he played for Wales, they were capable of matching anyone, as they showed in the 1958 World Cup. Welsh team manager Dave Bowen said of his selection sessions: 'I used to put the names of John Charles and Ivor Allchurch down and start from there.'

His versatility was endless: centre-forward, centre-half, midfield or even full-back; and he succeeded in two countries and two very different soccer environments. One manager used to say, when asked what position he would play Charles, if he were lucky enough to have him, 'Where I was weakest.'

Charles was admired by his co-professionals, respected by his opponents and held in awe by the fans. In Turin he received the film star treatment, unable to walk down a street without signing an autograph or being publicly applauded. '*Il Buon Gigante,*' the Gentle Giant, showed no temperament in the land of temperament, and was idolised for it.

Charles was never seen to commit a petty foul. He wrote in his autobiography: 'Players will have to realise that the public does not pay good money to see pettiness and childishness.'

Italian League Secretary, Luigi Scarambone, said in 1961, 'Wales should give him a medal. He's put it on the map. Nobody in Italy knew where or what it was before.'

Swansea-born Charles joined the ground-staff of his home-town club as soon as he was old enough but he didn't stay long. His talent was quickly spotted by Leeds manager, Major Frank Buckley and, still an amateur, he was persuaded to go to Elland Road.

During the course of the 1949-50 season, when he was an ever-present

John Charles

player in the Leeds side, Charles made his full international debut for Wales against Northern Ireland at Wrexham, thus becoming the youngest Welshman ever to represent his country; he was 18 years and 71 days old.

However, he did not win a regular place in the Welsh side until 1953. This came after the great transformation in his career, when Buckley decided to play him at centre-forward; the experiment quickly paid rich dividends, with 26 goals in his first season and then 42 in his second, to break the Leeds club record.

On 19 April, 1957, Charles was chosen as captain of Wales for the first time, for the match against Northern Ireland in Belfast. In the crowd that day was Umberto Agnelli, wealthy president of Juventus, and so began one of the most talked about transfers of all-time.

Within a week of the Belfast international, Leeds United and Agnelli had agreed terms. It took Charles a little longer, months of negotiation, in fact, but he signed in August, in time for the start of the Italian season, and for the sort of money players from the Football League had only dreamed about up to that moment. It was all cloak and dagger stuff but, eventually, Juventus paid £65,000, a record fee for a British player.

Within twelve months, a poll by the Italian football paper *Il Calcio Illustrato* elected Charles the best player in the country, and put his value at about £280,000; he was more highly rated then than di Stefano. Charles enjoyed it all. He bought a share in a restaurant, acquired a villa on the Italian Riviera, as well as one in Turin, and he had two cars.

Helped by the Welshman's 28 goals, Juventus won the Championship that year and, two years later, won both the Championship and the Cup, reaching a record 55 points and scoring 92 goals, with Charles just as much a provider, scoring 23 of them.

In the 1958 World Cup Finals in Sweden, John Charles was at centre-forward position in the Wales team that drew with Hungary, Mexico and Sweden before beating Hungary in a play-off and reaching the quarter-finals, but he was absent from the side that lost 1-0 to Brazil, the eventual winners.

Charles sang on records and made a film, but Juventus began to clamp down on his personal appearances, saying they were affecting his game. He was fined by the club for returning a day late from holiday with his family, and his home life suffered at the hands of the club's rigorous training schedules. Tired of manufactured press reports of a non-existent night life, the trouble came to a head at the time of his brief return to Leeds and his equally brief career with Roma afterwards.

One offer to return to his native land was from Southern League Barry Town, who would have paid £50 a week, as they were not bound by the Football League's maximum wage.

The negotiations on his leaving Juventus were more protracted than his original signature had been, and it took from April 1962 until August for it to be settled that Leeds would pay the Italians £53,000 for his return.

With Leeds he was an immediate attraction, but by November he had been sold back to Italy again, this time to Roma, at a fat profit for the Yorkshire club, not to mention a good one for Charles.

Sadly, injuries and a loss of form limited his appearances; he was dropped by Wales and finally signed for Cardiff. For a time, the Football League refused to accept his resignation because of money still owed to Leeds by Roma and Juventus.

It was obvious, too, that his greatest playing days were past and, after a short spell with the Bluebirds, he was transferred to Hereford United. He left Edgar Street less than a year before the club attained their ambition of League status and before the stunning run in the FA Cup.

By 1972, Charles was on the periphery of soccer, puzzled and saddened by the lack of demand for his services. He left his country as he was approaching his peak and his fans never saw the best, just the promise and the aftermath, and though he performed before the advent of the television era, legends outlive men, and John Charles certainly cannot erase his mark from the annals of the game.

One of the finest inside-forwards to appear in post-war football, **Ivor Allchurch** was a distinguished schemer, who played on either the right or left, and who appeared in over 700 first-class games. A goal-scorer, too, he was deadly within shooting range and scored over 250 goals.

During the time that he was an amateur at the Vetch Field, there were occasions when scouts from a number of top Football League clubs tried to persuade him to sign for them when he turned sixteen, but each time he refused, saying that he and his father had given their word that he would sign for Swansea Town.

On reaching his 18th birthday, he was enlisted in the Army as a gunner, but once his prowess as a footballer was recognised, he spent much of his time playing the game he loved so dearly. Based at Oswestry, he 'guested' for Shrewsbury and Wellington Town, as well as playing for his unit, the Western Command and the Army, often playing in three games a week.

Back at the Vetch, Allchurch found himself a member of a Swansea side that was struggling to make an impact on Division Two. Despite the club's lack of success, interest continued in the possibility of other clubs signing the 'Welsh Wizard'.

Ivor Allchurch

He made his international debut in November 1950, against England at Roker Park, after just 30 Football League appearances. As early as 1951, in just his seventh game for Wales, he helped his country celebrate its 75th Anniversary as a footballing nation by scoring twice against the Rest of the United Kingdom at Ninian Park. Whilst playing for his country, he was constantly being urged by his team-mates to move to a First Division club. There were also rumours that he would follow Eddie Firmani and move to an Italian club.

During the 1958 World Cup Finals, Wales beat Hungary 2-1, in a match in which Ivor Allchurch scored one of the greatest goals that many in the press box had ever seen. Receiving a long, lobbed pass from John Charles, he hit it on the volley, with his left foot, past a static Grosics in the Hungarian goal. This great equaliser was the turning point of the match. Three days later, Wales played Brazil in the quarter-final and, though they went down 1-0, Allchurch had found his true level. Some thought him the best inside-forward in the tournament.

Following Terry Medwin's move to Spurs, a number of the Swansea players, Allchurch among them, asked to be put on the transfer list. The 'Golden Boy' of Welsh soccer also decided to resign the captaincy of the club, in order to concentrate on his own fitness and form, before he joined Newcastle United, in October 1958, for a club record fee of £28,000.

In a fading team, he became a great favourite, playing in the famous black and white striped shirt, at St James' Park, which was regularly filled with the most passionate and appreciative crowd in the British game. He gave the Magpies four years of excellent service before returning to Wales to play for Cardiff City.

Bluebirds fans soon grew to love this ageing star as he displayed a more complete game than ever before, even scoring a hat-trick in Cardiff's 5-0 demolition of Swansea.

In May 1966, Allchurch, now back with Swansea, played his 68th and last game for Wales, in Chile, a record which stood for twenty years, until Joey Jones overtook him. The Queen presented him with the MBE for his services to football, and, in 1967-68, his last season of League football, he netted his seventh hat-trick as the Swans beat Doncaster Rovers. Allchurch, who was then 38, ended the campaign as the club's leading scorer, with 21 goals.

On leaving the Vetch Field for a second time, he played non-League football for a number of clubs, and played local football into his 50th year, when he was employed as a store-man.

Terry Medwin proved himself a very versatile forward with Swansea Town, occupying all the front line positions and, when he left the Vetch Field to join Tottenham Hotspur, he had already played three times for Wales and scored 60 goals for the Swans. During his last season with Swansea, Medwin scored 16 goals from the centre-forward berth and, although he did not play in that position for Spurs, he will always be best remembered at White Hart Lane as a fast, dangerous winger with immense power in both feet and the ability to whip in telling crosses with either foot.

His First Division form for Spurs soon earned him a recall to the Wales side, when he scored in a 2-2 draw with Scotland. During the 1958 World Cup, he was, without doubt, one of Wales's success stories and, in the vital play-off match against Hungary, he scored the winning goal.

Having scored two goals on his Spurs debut against Preston North End, Medwin had become a first team regular, as either winger or inside-forward, when he was struck down by a stomach bug in the autumn of 1960, and lost his place to Terry Dyson. Though he returned towards the end of the season to help Spurs win the League Championship, he was missing from the Cup Final side as the North London club completed the 'double'. However, he was in the Spurs side the following season when the club retained the FA Cup by beating Burnley 3-1.

Unfortunately, there was further drama to come for Medwin, for in the summer of 1963, he broke his leg on a close season tour of South Africa. After a long fight to regain full fitness, he eventually admitted defeat and retired to become manager of Athenian League side, Enfield. He later continued to work in football as a coach and scout, until ill-health forced his premature retirement in 1983.

Roy Vernon was a footballer of sublime talent, who made a colossal contribution to one of Everton's great sides. Yet he turned down the invitation of a trial with the Goodison club and opted to join the ground-staff of Blackburn Rovers. In his early days at Ewood Park, Vernon retained his amateur status so that he could represent Wales at both youth and amateur level, and he was only 19 when he won the first of 32 full caps for his country as Wales played out a goalless draw against Northern Ireland.

A member of Wales's 1958 World Cup Finals squad, he was also fiery and prone to rebellion. Despite having helped Rovers win promotion to the First Division in 1957-58, he clashed continually with new manager, Dally Duncan, and, in February 1960, he followed his mentor, Johnny Carey, to Everton.

The Blues' boss had, of course, encountered the Vernon temperament during his spell in charge at Blackburn, but was ready to weigh the outstanding gifts of an established international against non-footballing considerations.

On his arrival at Goodison, Vernon set about his work with compelling efficiency, heading the club's scoring charts in each of his four complete seasons on Merseyside. He also skippered the side to the 1962-63 League Championship, which he clinched with a hat-trick against Fulham, on the final day of the season.

There were, naturally, occasional brushes with Carey's successor, Harry Catterick, who made Vernon captain in the hope that the responsibility would both mellow and mature him. Yet, even so, the errant striker was sent home from a tour of the United States for breaking a curfew. However, a minor indiscretion such as this could never diminish the long-term stature of Roy Vernon. Those lucky enough to remember him in his prime would recall his beating off three defenders, over the space of five yards, before netting the ball, when at home to Arsenal in April 1961, and his deceiving of two Wolves defenders with one deft touch, before freeing Alex Young with a perfectly-weighted through ball, at Molineux in October 1962, and, of course, there were numerous penalties, driven with great power and accuracy past the reach of the hapless keeper.

Unfortunately for Everton fans, he continued to be less than enamoured with Catterick's disciplinary regime and, in March 1965, he left to join Stoke City.

Vernon proclaimed at the time that he would 'do a Bobby Collins' for his new club, referring to the little Scotsman's achievements after leaving for Leeds, and though that proved to be an unrealistic ambition, he did spend five generally productive years with the Potters. After a short time playing in South Africa, he was later reunited with former Blackburn team-mates, Bryan

Roy Vernon

Douglas and Ronnie Clayton, at Great Harwood. This might have been an incongruous setting for one of Wales's finest post-war strikers, but he and his former colleagues took the little Northern Premier League club into the first round of the FA Cup for the first time in its history. He later ran an antique business in Blackburn, but began to suffer with arthritis of the hip and spine and this resulted in his death at the early age of 56, in December 1993.

Ron Davies was one of the most consistent post-war goal-scorers; indeed, no forward has scored more First Division goals for Southampton than the Holywell-born striker and, for a spell, whilst he was at The Dell, he was justly regarded as the finest centre-forward in Europe. His career started at Chester in 1959, and it was there that Davies was made to hurdle, wearing army boots, training which he later claimed gave him extra power when jumping for crosses.

His travels took him to Luton and Norwich before Saints signed him for a record £55,000 in the summer of 1966.

Davies was already an established Welsh international but most Southampton fans did not expect him to make the immediate impact that he did. The south coast club was about to embark on its first season in the top flight, and Davies scored 37 goals in 41 games, to top the goal-scoring charts. With crosses from Paine and Sydenham floating in, Davies dominated the aerial battles and, along with George Best, he again headed the scoring charts for 1967-68.

A big but amiable giant, Davies was useful on the ground, but it was in the air that he inflicted most damage, although in Terry Paine he was lucky to have such a fine crosser of the ball. His success with the Saints turned him into a new commodity for his country. During the Home International Tournament of 1969, with three spectacular headers, Davies really established himself as a striker of true international worth.

However, on the domestic front, many top clubs learned how to cope with Davies's aerial power and his scoring was reduced somewhat, although he never gave less than his best. Towards the end of his career at The Dell, he began to suffer from a series of injuries, sustained from too many robust tackles, and he was unable to command a regular first team place.

He moved to rivals Portsmouth, before Manchester United, remembering his performances against them, surprised the football world by taking him to Old Trafford. Though he never started a game for the Reds, he did make a number of substitute appearances before ending his first-class career with Millwall.

A talented artist, who often drew caricatures of his colleagues, he now lives in Florida, where he coaches the Orlando Lions as well as giving private tuition to football-crazy youngsters.

Ron Davies

Much-travelled centre-forward **Wyn Davies** became affectionately known at Bolton as 'Wyn the Leap', due to his amazing heading talents. He had started his Football League career with Wrexham, playing in the Robins' famous League Cup run of 1960, and, in his last match before signing for the Wanderers, he was one of three players who scored a hat-trick in a 10-1 win over Hartlepool United.

Whilst with Bolton, he won the first of 34 full Welsh caps, his performances leading to his name being linked with a number of top flight clubs. He had scored 74 goals in 170 games for the Wanderers when, in October 1966, after a long chase and contest with Manchester City, he signed for Newcastle United.

Davies immediately became a crowd favourite. Though he cost the black and whites a record fee of £80,000, the big Welshman repaid the amount several times over. Although he never became one of the Magpies' goal-scoring machines, his contribution to United's cause for five years, as the club stormed Europe, was immense and it made him a cult hero on Tyneside.

He led Newcastle's line like few before or since, with ability to hold up the ball and bring his partners, notably Bryan 'Pop' Robson, into play. Davies created space for others and Robson, in particular, flourished as a top goal-getter. Davies was also able to soak up a physical battering by defenders, especially from foreign opposition who could not handle him at all.

Wyn Davies was one of the game's bravest players and, on many occasions, he soldiered on even though injured and in pain. Though he was not the best individual with the ball at his feet, Wyn Davies will always be recalled with esteem by every Newcastle supporter who witnessed his wholehearted displays. He was the key factor in United's Inter Cities Fairs Cup victory in 1969, and remains the club's top goal-scorer in European football, with ten goals.

Following an injury, he found it difficult to get back into the Newcastle side, and he returned to the north-west, to play for his long-standing admirer, Joe Mercer, at Manchester City. His stay at Maine Road was brief, and he moved across the city, to play for Manchester United. His hope of an Indian summer disappeared with the appointment of Tommy Docherty as manager, and he left to play for Blackpool. There followed spells with Crystal Palace and Stockport County before he ended his first-class career with Crewe Alexandra. After playing non-League football for Bangor City, he turned out for Arcadia Shepherds in the South African National League, before returning to work as a baker in Bolton.

Wyn Davies

One of the greatest names in Welsh soccer history, **John Toshack** was the youngest player to appear in a League match for Cardiff City, when he came off the bench, on 13 November 1965, to score the final goal in a 3-1 win over Leyton Orient; he was just 16 years 236 days old.

He was already an established international when Liverpool paid a then club record fee of £110,000 to take Toshack to Anfield. He soon endeared himself to the Kop when the Reds beat Everton in the Merseyside derby. In one of the most rousing of meetings, Toshack helped to erase a two-goal deficit, climbing high above the Blues' Brian Labone to head the equaliser, before nodding down Alec Lindsay's cross for Chris Lawler to clinch an emotional victory.

Though he was always a power in the air, other aspects of his game were in need of serious attention. He applied himself well and gradually acquired more all-round skills, of which accurate distribution was the most notable. He was also blessed, for most of his Liverpool career, with the presence of Kevin Keegan, and the diverse talents of the towering Welshman and his nippy, opportunist partner combined to give the Anfield club many of their finest hours.

Toshack's improvement, which resulted in him laying on a steady stream of chances, with subtle flicks to his accomplice, and creating space by astute running off the ball, enabled him to play an important role in winning six major trophies. Yet, throughout most of his Anfield tenure, he was dogged by a nagging thigh injury, and only once did he exceed 30 League games in a campaign.

Toshack gave some of his best performances in the club's European matches. One of the most unexpected came in the 1972-73 UEFA Cup Final first leg, at home to Borussia Mönchengladbach, for which he had been omitted. The match was abandoned because of heavy rain, but manager Bill Shankly had spotted that the German players were vulnerable in the air. Accordingly, the Welsh target man was recalled for the rescheduled game and

John Toshack

laid on two goals for Keegan. His most prolific term for the Reds was 1975-76, when he found the net 23 times, including three hat-tricks, on the way to a League title and UEFA Cup double.

Thereafter, fitness problems and greater competition for places preceded a move, as player-manager, to Swansea where, with phenomenal success, the Swans climbed from the Fourth to the First Division in the space of three years. This put Toshack on a management trail which was to take him all the way to Real Madrid.

After taking charge of Sporting Lisbon, he managed Real Sociedad and, in his first season, he led them to victory over Athletico Madrid in the Spanish Cup Final. At Real Madrid, he guided them to the League Championship, with a record number of points and goals, yet this did not prevent him being sacked after an indifferent start to the following season.

In March 1994, Toshack had a spell as Welsh national team boss, but it lasted just 44 days and one game.

Ian Rush was a striker with a phenomenal work-rate, who put defenders under pressure and then picked up the pieces.

He began his career with Chester City but, after just one season at Sealand Road, having noted his potential, Liverpool moved to sign him, and before he even kicked a ball for the Reds, he received the first of 73 Welsh caps when he came on as a substitute during a 1-0 defeat at Hampden Park, against Scotland, in May 1980. He made no impact in his first season at Anfield, failing to score in seven end-of-season games. Out of favour at the start of the 1981-82 season, he went to see Bob Paisley about his future at the club and was told, 'Just score goals.' Deputising for the injured David Johnson that October, he netted twice in a 3-0 victory over Leeds United, and the rest, so to speak, is history, for he burst onto the First Division scene with 17 goals in 32 matches, ending the season with a League Cup winners' medal, after scoring the third goal in a 3-1 defeat of Tottenham Hotspur.

The next five seasons were honours all the way, except for 1984-85, with

Ian Rush

three League Cup wins, a European Cup winners' medal and an FA Cup winners' medal in 1986, after he had scored twice in a 3-1 victory over Everton. It was during this time that his partnership with Kenny Dalglish became legendary, but after repeated overtures from top Italian side, Juventus, he was transferred for a new English record fee during the 1987 close season.

He had been Liverpool's leading scorer in five of his six full seasons at Anfield and seemed to be almost impossible to replace, after scoring 207 goals in 331 matches.

Unfortunately, his time at Juventus was not a happy one, as the Italian's club coach expected him to forage alone. Nevertheless, although he scored eight goals in 29 games, a respectable total for the Italian League, he made little effort to acclimatise, and Juventus allowed him to rejoin Liverpool in the summer of 1988.

His first season back in the top flight was plagued by injury problems but he came back with a bang in the FA Cup Final against Everton when, as a substitute, he scored two of Liverpool's goals in a 3-2 extra-time win over their Mersey rivals.

In winning his fifth League Championship medal in 1989-90, he found the net 18 times and, in 1990-91, he again headed the club's scoring charts, with 16. Though he endured a miserable season in 1991-92, being absent through injury for much of the time, the following season seemed, at one time, likely to signal his departure from Anfield. However, it ended in a blaze of glory, with 11 goals in the last 13 games. During the early part of the season, he had scored four goals in the European Cup Winners Cup game against Apollon Limassol of Cyprus, to beat Roger Hunt's record of 18 in European competition, and had netted a hat-trick for Wales against the Faroe Isles a week before, to claim the all-time scoring record for his country.

In October 1992, he made his 500th appearance for Liverpool and struck his 200th Football League goal the following month. However, despite establishing new records every other week, his form in the Premier League was fitful and, midway through the season, manager Graeme Souness lost patience and dropped him for the first time in his Liverpool career. He returned as substitute in the following game, at home to Manchester United, and lashed in a magnificent equaliser. He then scored in six of the next seven games, while notching his 300th Liverpool goal in the process.

Towards the end of his Liverpool career, he became the club captain and, while he continued to score goals, he found time to coach the young Robbie Fowler.

One of Liverpool's finest-ever players, scoring 346 goals in 658 games (including European matches and friendlies), Rush joined Leeds United in May 1996. At Elland Road, he hit the worst goal-scoring drought of his career and, at the end of the season, he joined Newcastle United. With the Magpies he extended his record as the top FA goal-scorer of the twentieth century before, following a loan spell with Sheffield United, he joined Wrexham as their player-coach, leaving the Racecourse Ground in the summer of 1999.

Quicksilver striker **Dean Saunders** is the son of Roy who played for Liverpool and Swansea City between 1948 and 1963. He came into League football with Swansea City but was not highly regarded by manager John Bond, and was released on a free transfer, following a spell on loan at Cardiff City, and signed for Brighton and Hove Albion.

Immediately impressing the Seagulls' fans with 15 League goals in 1985-86, he was recognised by the Welsh manager and made his international debut against the Irish Republic in March 1986. Towards the end of the following season, he was sold to Oxford United, who were struggling at the foot of the First Division. He made an immediate impact, scoring six goals in 12 games and helping to secure United's status. However, at the end of the following season, Oxford were relegated to the Second Division and Saunders was sold to Derby County.

In three seasons at the Baseball Ground, he was the Rams' leading scorer and, in 1990-91, his 17 goals from 37 games was a remarkable achievement for

Dean Saunders

a team doomed to relegation almost from the start of the season.

Sold to Liverpool in the summer of 1991, for a record transfer fee between two English clubs of £2.9 million, he struggled to make an impact at Anfield, despite finishing as the club's leading scorer, with 23 goals in all competitions and collecting an FA Cup winners' medal.

In September 1992, he was transferred to Aston Villa for a sum £600,000 less than the Reds had paid for him. His first home game was, ironically, against Liverpool, when he scored two of the goals in a 4-2 victory and went on to become the club's leading goal-scorer, with 17 from all first team matches.

A striker who loved to have the ball in behind defenders, where he could use his pace to maximum effect, Saunders had three good seasons at Villa Park before leaving to join Turkish club Galatasaray in the summer of 1995.

He returned to the Football League a year later, when Nottingham Forest paid £1.5 million to secure his signature. Though his work-rate never faltered, he did not have the best of times at the City Ground and, in December 1997, he was allowed to move to Sheffield United on a free transfer.

He immediately proved his ability, scoring one of the best goals of the season, when volleying past the Port Vale keeper from the touch-line. Playing with great enthusiasm, his quick thinking and awareness were still in evidence when Benfica took advantage of a clause in his contract to sign him for £500,000.

After six months in Portugal, he returned to the Premiership with Bradford City and was a regular in the Bantams' line-up throughout the 1999-2000 campaign. Sadly, he then suffered a series of injuries, and had hamstring, knee and cartilage problems. Finding himself out of contract, Saunders, the most capped outfield player for Wales, left Valley Parade in the summer of 2001.

Current Welsh team manager **Mark Hughes** was a striker who was as strong as an ox and skilful as well. Bringing maximum pressure to bear in opponents' penalty areas, when tackling defenders, he made chances for others, as well as being a proficient goal-scorer himself.

Hughes began his career with Manchester United and, by the end of 1983-84, he was a regular front runner. His progress was recognised internationally when he was selected to play for Wales against England in May 1984 and, in a dream debut for his country, he scored the only goal of the game at his home-town ground, Wrexham.

In 1984-85, his first full season, he was the club's leading scorer, with 24 League goals, and was prominent when United triumphed 1-0 in the FA Cup Final against Everton. Although finding goals harder to come by in the following season, he was still the subject of a £2.5 million bid from the Spanish giants, Barcelona, managed by Terry Venables, who eventually signed him to link-up with Gary Lineker.

However, the Spanish fans didn't seem to appreciate Hughes's ability to make space for other players with his unselfish running off the ball. His stay in Spain was less than successful and, following a brief spell in Germany, on loan with Bayern Munich, he returned to old Trafford in the summer of 1988.

The season was generally a disappointing one for both him and United, though there was consolation in 1990, when the Reds beat Crystal Palace 1-0 in a replay, to win the FA Cup Final, after the teams had drawn 3-3 in the first match. The six-goal thriller had been a personal triumph, when he put United ahead on the hour and then equalised with just seven minutes of extra-time remaining.

With that victory, United returned to European competition, when the ban on English clubs was finally lifted. United reached the European Cup Winners Cup Final in Rotterdam, to face Hughes's former club, Barcelona. The Reds fully deserved their 2-1 victory and Hughes's goal, a tremendous shot on the run from a tight angle, clinched the victory. In some sources, he is

Mark Hughes

credited with United's first goal, although he only touched Bruce's already goal-bound header over the line.

He was voted by his fellow professionals as the 1991 PFA 'Player of the Year', an award he had previously won in 1989. During 1991-92, he helped United win the League Cup for the first time, and then was instrumental in the Reds winning the Premiership in 1992-93 and 1993-94. He had another outstanding season in 1994-95, despite constant speculation regarding his future. In February 1995, he signed a new two-year contract, much to the delight of the United faithful, but the following summer he was sold to Chelsea for a fee of £1.5 million.

At Stamford Bridge, 'Sparky' proved that he was still the best target man in the business, particularly with his back to goal. Although his muscular approach made life difficult for defenders, it also incurred the wrath of referees, and he suffered two lengthy suspensions during the season. In 1996-97, Hughes played some of the best football of his career. He formed an almost telepathic understanding with Gianfranco Zola but, despite hitting top form, he was left on the bench for the pulsating fourth round FA Cup tie at home to Liverpool. At half-time, with the Blues 2-0 down, Ruud Gullit brought Hughes off the bench and, within five minutes, he had reduced the deficit with a typical Hughes goal. Leading the line magnificently, his sheer physical presence lifted the team as they completed a remarkable comeback to win 4-2. He continued his great record in the FA Cup, helping the Blues reach their fifth final before creating a 20th century record with his fourth FA Cup winners' medal following the 2-0 victory over Middlesborough.

Voted Chelsea's 'Player of the Year', Hughes scored against his old club, Manchester United, in the Charity Shield at Wembley, and scored against the Reds again. It was his first goal at Old Trafford since his move to Chelsea.

He then received the award that rounded off an incredible year for him: he was awarded the MBE in the New Year's Honours List for his services to football.

After helping Chelsea beat Stuttgart in the final of the European Cup Winners Cup, Hughes joined Southampton, in the knowledge that he had more chance of playing regular first team football at The Dell than at Stamford Bridge. In the event, he actually made more appearances in midfield than he did as a striker, where his strength on the ball and ability to resist challenges were a great asset as the Saints fought to avoid relegation.

He was put in temporary charge of the Welsh national side in June 1999 and confirmed as manager some five months later.

Though he was content to combine his new job with that of a Southampton player, he left The Dell and moved north in response to an Everton injury crisis. He soon showed that the passing years had not dimmed his appetite for a physical tussle, and went on to produce some memorable displays in some of the club's biggest matches, notably the Merseyside derby against Liverpool.

In October 2000, he was on the move again, this time to Blackburn Rovers and, after helping them win promotion to the Premiership, was a member of the side that won the League Cup at Cardiff's Millennium Stadium.

Now, having come to the end of a fine playing career, he has begun to demonstrate his capabilities as a manager as Wales have again become a force to be reckoned with at international level.

Selecting a best Wales side is a fascinating exercise but the results are bound to be highly subjective. Of course, different players reached their best in different decades, and comparisons can be odious. The more I thought about all the players who have represented Wales, the more difficult the task of selecting my best Welsh side became.

How good a player is, or has been, is purely a matter of opinion, and I am sure not everyone will agree with my team of Welsh Football Heroes, for it certainly was not easy to omit players of the calibre of Jack Kelsey, Trevor Ford and Mark Hughes.

Why not compare my team with yours:

Neville Southall
Alf Sherwood
Mel Hopkins
Fred Keenor
Mike England
Kevin Ratcliffe
Billy Meredith
John Charles
Ian Rush
Ivor Allchurch
Ryan Giggs

At the time of writing, Mark Hughes's Welsh revolution took another step forward when his side pulled off a stunning win in Helsinki, to get the Euro 2004 campaign off to a flying start, and then followed it with a victory over mighty Italy.

The way Hughes has got his side playing, the prospect of reaching a first major championship finals for 46 years has every chance of becoming a reality.

Who knows, if this book were being written in a few years' time, then players such as Craig Bellamy and Simon Davies, among others, would have every chance of being included.

**– Wales within your reach:
an attractive series
at attractive prices!**

Titles already published:

1. Welsh Talk
Heini Gruffudd
086243 447 5
£2.95

2. Welsh Dishes
Rhian Williams
086243 492 0
£2.95

3. Welsh Songs
Lefi Gruffudd (ed.)
086243 525 0
£3.95

4. Welsh Mountain Walks
Dafydd Andrews
086243 547 1
£3.95

5. Welsh Organic Recipes
Dave and Barbara Frost
086243 574 9
£3.95

6. Welsh Railways
Jim Green
086243 551 X
£3.95

7. Welsh Place Names
Brian Davies
086243 514 5
£3.95

8. Welsh Castles
Geraint Roberts
086243 550 1
£3.95

9. Welsh Rugby Heroes
Androw Bennett
086243 552 8
£3.95

10. Welsh National Heroes
Alun Roberts
086243 610 9
£4.95

11. Welsh Fun and Games
Ethne Jefferys
086243 627 3
£4.95

12. Welsh Jokes
Dilwyn Phillips
086243 619 2
£3.95

The *It's Wales* series
is just one of a wide range
Welsh interest publications
from Y Lolfa.
For a full list of books currently in print,
send now for your free copy
of our new, full-colour Catalogue
– or simply surf into our website
at **www.ylolfa.com**.

Talybont Ceredigion Cymru/*Wales* SY24 5AP
ffôn 0044 (0)1970 832 304 *ffacs* 832 782 *isdn* 832 813
e-bost ylolfa@ylolfa.com *y we* www.ylolfa.com